CENTRE FOR INFORMATION ON THE
TEACHING OF ENGLISH

EXHIBITION STOCK

RETURN TO

MORAY HOUSE COLLEGE OF EDUCATION

MAN
Book One

His Senses

MAN

Book One: His Senses

Book Two: Looking around Him

Book Three: Looking at Himself

Editors

Charles Gardiner   Headmaster of Intake County
                     Secondary School, Leeds

John Glen   Headmaster of Swarcliffe County
                     Primary School, Leeds

Rita Scully   Headmistress of Frizinghill Junior
                     and Infant School, Bradford

12-inch long-playing gramophone records
of poems from each of these books are
obtainable from the publishers.

MAN

I

His Senses

Edited by *Charles Gardiner*, *John Glen*, *Rita Scully*

GEORGE G. HARRAP & CO. LTD
*London * Toronto * Wellington * Sydney*

First published in Great Britain 1971
by GEORGE G. HARRAP & Co. LTD
182–184 High Holborn, London W.C.1V 7AX

© *Charles Gardiner, John Glen, Rita Scully* 1971

ISBN 0 245 50408 7

*Composed in Monotype Garamond type and printed
by Western Printing Services Ltd, Bristol
Made in Great Britain*

Acknowledgments

Thanks are due to the following for kind permission to print the poems included in this anthology:

Barrie and Jenkins Ltd, for 'London Spring' by Frances Cornford; Chatto and Windus Ltd, for 'Smelling The End of Green July' from *Light and Dark* by Peter Yates; the Clarendon Press, Oxford, for 'The Winnowers' from *The Poetical Works of Robert Bridges*; Constable and Co Ltd, for 'The Autumn Wind' from *One Hundred and Seventy Chinese Poems* by Arthur Waley; Mrs H. M. Davies, for 'The Rain' and 'The Fog' from *The Complete Poems of W. H. Davies* (Jonathan Cape Ltd); J. M. Dent and Sons Ltd, and the Trustees for the Copyrights of the late Dylan Thomas, for 'Fern Hill' from *Collected Poems*, and for extract from *Under Milk Wood*; J. M. Dent and Sons, for extract from 'The Emigrants' from *First Day* by Clifford Dyment; Andre Deutsch Ltd, for 'Apples' from *My Many Coated Man* by Laurie Lee; A. Elliott-Cannon, for 'Fish and Chips'; the Estate of Robert Frost, for 'The Line Gang' from *The Poetry of Robert Frost* edited by Edward Connery Latham (Jonathan Cape Ltd); Essex Music Ltd, for 'If I had a Hammer' by Lee Hays and Pete Seeger; The Executors of the James Joyce Estate, for 'All day I hear the noise of waters' from *Chamber Music* by James Joyce (Jonathan Cape Ltd); Faber and Faber Ltd, for 'Prelude' and 'New Hampshire' from *Collected Poems 1909–1962* by T. S. Eliot, and for 'Echo' from *Collected Poems* by Lawrence Durrell; Michael Gibson and Macmillan Co. Ltd, for 'Hands' from *Collected Poems* by W. W. Gibson; John Goodger, for 'After School'; The Hardy Estate, The Macmillan Company of Canada, and Macmillan and Co, for 'Snow in the Suburbs' by Thomas Hardy; Houghton Mifflin Company, for 'Dolphins in Bluewater' from *The Complete Poetical Works of Amy Lowell*; Linda Hughes, for 'The National English Meal'; Carl Inglis, for 'Eclipse'; J. A. Lindon and *Envoi*, for 'There are More Things'; The Literary Trustees of Walter de la Mare and The Society of Authors, for 'The Song of Shadows' by Walter de la Mare; The Macmillan Co, New York, for 'Swift Things are Beautiful' from *Poems of Praise* by Elizabeth Coatsworth; Charles Martin, for 'The Wound'; Methuen and Co Ltd, for 'Smells', from *Chimney Smoke* by Christopher Morley; Peter Mullineaux, for 'Harvest Festival'; John Murray Ltd, for 'Man' from *Philosophies* by Sir Ronald Ross; Hubert Nicholson, for 'Radio' by A. S. J. Tessimond; Oxford University Press, for 'Pied Beauty' and 'Inversnaid' from *Poems of Gerard Manley Hopkins*; Rita Peck and *Envoi*, for 'The Blue Door'; A. D. Peters and Co, for 'Underground' from *Modern Verse for Town Boys and Girls* by Rose Macaulay (Clarendon Press), for 'Food on Board Ship' from *Sonnets and Verse* by Hilaire Belloc (Gerald Duckworth and Co. Ltd); and for 'In Lamplight' from *Collected Poems* by Martin Armstrong (Martin Secker and Warburg); R. J. Pickles, for 'Mad Cat'; D. O. Pitches and Breakthru Publications, for 'Wind Through Barley'; Lawrence Pollinger Ltd and the Estate of the late Mrs Frieda Lawrence, for 'Bare Almond Trees', 'Bavarian Gentians', and 'Things Men Have Made' from *The Complete Poems of D. H. Lawrence* (William Heinemann Ltd); Lawrence Pollinger Ltd, for 'Who Whistled?' from *The Collected Poems of Richard Church* (William Heinemann Ltd); Joan Prince for 'Alarm'; *Punch* and The Hamlyn Publishing Group, for 'Noise' by Jessie Pope; Sidgwick and Jackson Ltd, for 'Morning Thanksgiving' from *The Collected Poems of John Drinkwater*; The Society of Authors, representatives for the Estate of John Masefield, for 'Dawn' by John Masefield; Stephen Tasker, for 'Sound'; John Walsh, for 'Under the Pier' and 'The Anemone'; Mrs Iris Wise, The Macmillan Company of Canada, and Macmillan and Co Ltd, for 'When you walk in a field' by James Stephens; Barbara Woods, for 'The Head'; M. B. Yeats and Macmillan and Co, for 'The Wild Swans at Coole' from *The Collected Poems of W. B. Yeats*; The *Yorkshire Evening Post*, for 'Blue' by Susan Goss, and 'Time Stood Still' by John Woolley.

The cover design is by Ian Gliddon; the photographs, specially commissioned, were taken by Gareth Bowen.

Contents

7

8

Man

Sir Ronald Ross

Man putteth the world to scale
   And weigheth out the stars;
Th'eternal hath lost her veil,
   The infinite her bars;
His balance he hath hung in heaven
   And set the sun therein.

Prelude

T. S. Eliot

The winter evening settled down
With smell of steaks in passageways.
Six o'clock.
The burnt-out ends of smoky days.
And now a gusty shower wraps
The grimy scraps
Of withered leaves about your feet
And newspapers from vacant lots;
The showers beat
On broken blinds and chimney pots,
And at the corner of the street
A lonely cab-horse steams and stamps.
And then the lighting of the lamps.

David's Song from 'Saul'

Robert Browning

Oh, our manhood's prime vigour! No spirit feels waste,
Not a muscle is stopped in its playing, nor sinew unbraced.
Oh, the wild joys of living! the leaping from rock up to rock,
The strong rending of boughs from the fir-tree, the cool silver
    shock
Of the plunge in a pool's living water,—the hunt of the bear,
And the sultriness showing the lion is couched in his lair.
And the meal, the rich dates yellowed over with gold dust
    divine,
And the locust's flesh steeped in the pitcher; the full draught
    of wine,
And the sleep in the dried river-channel where bulrushes tell
That the water was wont to go warbling so softly and well.
How good is man's life, the mere living! how fit to employ
All the heart and the soul and the senses, for ever in joy!

Pied Beauty

Gerard Manley Hopkins

Glory be to God for dappled things—
For skies of couple-colour as a brindled cow;
For rose-moles all in stipple upon trout that swim;
Fresh firecoal chestnut-falls; finches' wings
Landscape plotted and pieced—fold, fallow, and plough;
And all trades, their gear and tackle and trim.

All things counter, original, spare, strange;
Whatever is fickle, freckled (who knows how?)
With swift, slow; sweet, sour; a dazzle, dim;
He fathers-forth whose beauty is past change:
      Praise Him.

From: 'The Great Lover'

Rupert Brooke

These I have loved:
  White plates and cups, clean-gleaming,
Ringed with blue lines; and feathery, faery dust;
Wet roofs, beneath the lamp-light; the strong crust
Of friendly bread; and many-tasting food;
Rainbows; and the blue bitter smoke of wood;
And radiant raindrops couching in cool flowers;
And flowers themselves, that sway through sunny hours,
Dreaming of moths that drink them under the moon;
Then, the cool kindliness of sheets, that soon
Smooth away trouble; and the rough male kiss
Of blankets; grainy wood; live hair that is
Shining and free; blue-massing clouds, the keen
Unpassioned beauty of a great machine;
The benison of hot water; furs to touch;
The good smell of old clothes; and other such—
The comfortable smell of friendly fingers,
Hair's fragrance, and the musty reek that lingers
About dead leaves and last year's ferns. . . .

                              Dear names,
And thousand other throng to me! Royal flames;
Sweet water's dimpling laugh from tap or spring;
Holes in the ground; and voices that do sing;
Voices in laughter, too; and body's pain,
Soon turned to peace; and the deep-panting train;
Firm sands; the little dulling edge of foam
That browns and dwindles as the wave goes home;
And washen stones, gay for an hour; the cold
Graveness of iron; moist black earthen mould;
Sleep, and high places; footprints in the dew;
And oaks; and brown horse-chestnuts, glossy-new;
And new-peeled sticks; and shining pools on grass;—
All these have been my loves.

Inversnaid

Gerard Manley Hopkins

This darksome burn, horseback brown,
His rollrock highroad roaring down,
In coop and in comb the fleece of his foam
Flutes and low to the lake falls home.

A windpuff-bonnet of fawn-froth
Turns and twindles over the broth
Of a pool so pitchblack, fell-frowning,
It rounds and rounds Despair to drowning.

Degged with dew, dappled with dew
Are the groins of the braes that the brook treads through,
Wiry heathpacks, flitches of fern,
And the beadbonny ash that sits over the burn.

What would the world be, once bereft
Of wet and of wildness? Let them be left,
O let them be left, wildness and wet;
Long live the weeds and the wilderness yet.

Blue

Susan Goss
(aged 9)

The light blue of the sky,
   The dark blue of the sea,
Bluebells in the garden
   Picked by you and me.

The blue of my jumper,
   The blue of my toys,
The blue of the faces
   Of cold little boys.

Time Stood Still

John Woolley

Time stood still.
No will
No length
No strength
  Just Eternity.

'Tick . . . Tack . . . Tick . . . Tack . . . Tock!'
Beat the solitary clock,
Unheeded,
Not needed.

No wind,
No rain,
No lilting tune,
No soft refrain.

Oppressive silence, as heavy as lead.
All dead.
   Eternity.

The Wild Swans at Coole

W. B. Yeats

The trees are in their autumn beauty,
The woodland paths are dry,
Under the October twilight the water
Mirrors a still sky;
Upon the brimming water among the stones
Are nine-and-fifty swans.

The nineteenth autumn has come upon me
Since I first made my count;
I saw, before I had well finished,
All suddenly mount
And scatter, wheeling, in great broken rings
Upon their clamorous wings.

I have looked upon those brilliant creatures,
And now my heart is sore.
All's changed since I, hearing at twilight,
The first time on this shore,
The bell-beat of their wings above my head,
Trod with a lighter tread.

Unwearied still, lover by lover,
They paddle in the cold
Companionable streams or climb the air;
Their hearts have not grown old;
Passion or conquest, wander where they will,
Attend upon them still.

The Blue Door - A Painting

Rita Peck

A blue door,
Tangled in leaves,
Shadowy blue
In a crumbling wall;
The quiet years
Have touched this door,
Till gauze of snow
And silvering of rain
Have smoothed and softened
Its lacquered brightness.
Under summer's amber hands
It faded, blue on blue
To water tints of turquoise,
Coral, jade, and sapphire.

A blue door,
No longer dominant,
Metallic;
But soft as flame.
Blue so subtle
Thoughts slide through it
Into forest worlds;
This door once tree
Is tree again.
Into its fountaining life
Vitality passes,
Music is all around.
Woodwind sweet,
The great trees sing,
And blue, blue, blue
As frosty flame,
As hyacinth hollows
Fall the long leaf shadows—

Through this blue door
The widening universe of beauty
Falls away in singing fathoms
Of delicious light,
Windless,
Secret.

There are More Things

J. A. Lindon

On the dim web-clustered wall thin fingers run
 Silent and swift,
Drop to the floor and scuttle, beetle-loud,
Over the dingy boards beneath the humped
Slumped figure moulded by the quilt.
 A probing gust
 Ponders the window-catch.
Spilt quicksilver and lead spatter the room.
 An owlet shrieks.
 Festoons of downy dust
Sway by the pale rectangle where a tattered cloud
 Strangles the moon.
 Great weeds of darkness drift.
 A dull board creaks.

Something is forming in the womb-like patch
Of wool-black shadow where the curtains rise,
Something obscene, malignant, infamous,
Born of the terrified and shrinking air,
 Fœtal and hideous,
 Foul as a cobweb, chill as frost,
 Mute as a muffled nun,
 Something with blind, blank, evil eyes
 Is forming there,
And the sleeper lost,
 Lies unaware.

A Memory

William Allingham

Four ducks on a pond,
A grass-bank beyond,
A blue sky of spring,
White clouds on the wing:
What a little thing
To remember for years—
To remember with tears!

The Shell

Alfred Lord Tennyson

See what a lovely shell,
Small and pure as a pearl,
Lying close to my foot,
Frail, but a work divine,
Made so fairily well
With delicate spire and whorl,
How exquisitely minute,
A miracle of design!

Echo

Lawrence Durrell

Nothing is lost, sweet self,
Nothing is ever lost.
The unspoken word
Is not exhausted but can be heard.
Music that stains
The silence remains
O echo is everywhere, the unbeckonable bird!

Noise

Jessie Pope

I like noise.
The whoop of a boy, the thud of a hoof,
The rattle of rain on a galvanized roof,
The hubbub of traffic, the roar of a train,
The throb of machinery numbing the brain,
The switching of wires in an overhead tram,
The rush of the wind, a door on the slam,
The boom of the thunder, the crash of the waves,
The din of a river that races and raves,
The crack of a rifle, the clank of a pail,
The strident tattoo of a swift-slapping sail—
From any old sound that the silence destroys
Arises a gamut of soul-stirring joys.
I like noise.

Sound

Stephen Tasker
(aged 16)

What sounds have entered into the
Minds of men down the eardrums of
Time and left a doubt, or a conviction?

Laughter, loud and gay, trickling
From the lips of young children, or
Exploding like bombs from the toothless
Mouths of the aged.
The drip of a tap, sure and steady
Saying 'Rest—all's well—water flows
Why worry?'
The snarl of a sabre-toothed
Motor bike, hunted, captured, and tamed
By unproved manhood.
The click of steel stiletto heels on a
Cobbled street, denying for ever
The soft femininity of
Their wearer's feet.
The tramp of many footbeats—communal
Singing—a lonely white whistle
In the night.

Music—the blaring
Wrench of an orchestra, or the
Delicate embroidery of a flute.
An organ, humming its message to a
Dead church.

Words—my greatest love.
Delicate or harsh
Forcing the lips into
Poetry or pornography.

Sounds of pain—an animal
Singing its death to parasite ears.

Or a man singing his life.
Creaking of stubborn trunks
Which have yet to learn
The art of bending with
Relentless winds; or
Growing in the shade of nature's
Paternal hills.
The anguished cry of love.

Sounds of joy—the rustle of
Branches as winged lovers
Fly backwards and forwards
Preaching their creed to
All ears or no ears.
The ecstatic scream of
Love in embryo,
Or the explosion of
God, which comes with finding form.

Fetishistic noise,
Soaring, leaping, diving into
Aural ecstasy, demanding attention
Like an urgent boiling kettle.
Sounds to be remembered by the crawling
Python in my spine.

The Rain

W. H. Davies

I hear leaves drinking rain;
I hear rich leaves on top
Giving the poor beneath
Drop after drop;
'Tis a sweet noise to hear
These green leaves drinking near.

And when the Sun comes out,
After this rain shall stop,
A wondrous light will fill
Each dark, round drop;
I hope the Sun shines bright;
'Twill be a lovely sight.

The Splendour Falls

Alfred Lord Tennyson

The splendour falls on castle walls
And snowy summits old in story:
The long light shakes across the lakes,
And the wild cataract leaps in glory,
Blow, bugle, blow, set the wild echoes flying,
Blow, bugle; answer, echoes, dying, dying, dying.

O hark, O hear! how thin and clear,
And thinner, clearer, farther going!
O sweet and far from cliff and scar
The horns of Elfland faintly blowing!
Blow, let us hear the purple glens replying:
Blow, bugle; answer, echoes, dying, dying, dying.

O love, they die in yon rich sky,
They faint on hill or field or river:
Our echoes roll from soul to soul,
And grow for ever and for ever.
Blow, bugle, blow, set the wild echoes flying,
And answer, echoes, answer, dying, dying, dying.

Bavarian Gentians

D. H. *Lawrence*

Not every man has gentians in his house
in soft September, at slow, sad Michaelmas.

Bavarian gentians, big and dark, only dark
darkening the day-time torch-like with the smoking blueness of
    Pluto's gloom,
ribbed and torch-like, with their blaze of darkness spread blue
down flattening into points, flattened under the sweep of white
    day
torch-flower of the blue-smoking darkness, Pluto's dark-blue
    daze,
black lamps from the halls of Dis, burning dark-blue,
giving off darkness, blue darkness, as Demeter's pale lamps
    give off light,
lead me then, lead me the way.

Reach me a gentian, give me a torch
let me guide myself with the blue, forked touch of this flower
down the darker and darker stairs, where blue is darkened on
      blueness,
even where Persephone goes, just now, from the frosted
      September
to the sightless realm where darkness is awake upon the dark
and Persephone herself is but a voice
or a darkness invisible enfolded in the deeper dark
of the arms Plutonic, and pierced with the passion of dense
      gloom,
among the splendour of torches of darkness, shedding darkness
      on the lost bride and her groom.

I saw a peacock

Nursery Rhyme

I saw a peacock with a fiery tail
I saw a blazing comet drop down hail
I saw a cloud with ivy circled round
I saw a sturdy oak creep on the ground
I saw a pismire swallow up a whale
I saw a raging sea brim full of ale
I saw a Venice glass sixteen foot deep
I saw a well full of men's tears that weep
I saw their eyes all in a flame of fire
I saw a house as big as the moon and higher
I saw the sun even in the midst of night
I saw the man that saw this wondrous sight.

Turtle Soup

Lewis Carroll

Beautiful soup, so rich and green,
Waiting in a hot tureen!
Who for such dainties would not stoop?
Soup of the evening, beautiful SOUP!

Beau-ootiful Soo-oop!
Beau-ootiful Soo-oop!
Soo-oop of the e-e-evening,
Beautiful, beautiful Soup!

Beautiful Soup! Who cares for fish,
Game, or any other dish?
Who would not give all else for two
Pennyworth only of beautiful Soup?

Beau-ootiful Soo-oop!
Beau-ootiful Soo-oop!
Soo-oop of the e-e-evening,
Beautiful, beauti-FUL SOUP!

London Spring

Frances Cornford

The rounded buses loom through softest blue,
The pavement smells of dust and of narcissus too,
The awnings stretch like petals in the sun,
And even the oldest taxis glitter as they run.

Over the sooted secret garden walls
As in another Eden cherry-blossom falls,
Lithe under shadowing lilacs steal the cats
And even the oldest ladies tilt their summery hats.

All day I hear the noise of waters

James Joyce

All day I hear the noise of waters
Making moan,
Sad as the seabird is when going
Forth alone
He hears the winds cry to the waters'
Monotone.

The grey winds, the cold winds are blowing
Where I go.
I hear the noise of many waters
Far below.
All day, all night, I hear them flowing
To and fro.

Daybreak

R. L. Stevenson

On the gorgeous hills of morning
A sudden piping of birds,
A piping of all the forest, high and merry and clear,
I lay in my tent and listened;
I lay and heard them long,

In the dark of the moonlit morning,
The birds of the night at song.
I lay and listened and heard them
Sing ere the day was begun;
Sing and sink into
Silence one by one.
I lay in my bed and looked—
Paler than starlight or lightning
A glimmer. . . .

The Head

Barbara Woods

The head of a man, or maybe not:
more like an ape;
a quiet still figure.
The ears are like the mouth of a trumpet,
but crinkled at the edges.
The eyes are small and dead;
they frown, and look at you in scorn.
The face is square like a box,
somehow alive and strangely grotesque.
The head bald as an egg,
maybe through worry, and maybe fright.
His mouth is open;
he may be screaming; he may be singing,
but I cannot hear him.
His nose, like a boxer puppy's tail,
faces you defiantly,
never moving, like an oak tree.

The Autumn Wind

Arthur Waley

Autumn wind rises; white clouds fly.
Grass and trees wither; geese go south.
Orchids, all in bloom; chrysanthemums smell sweet;
I think of my lovely lady; I never can forget.
Floating-pagoda boat crosses Fen River;
Across the mid-stream white waves rise.
Flute and drum keep time to sound of rowers' song;
Amidst revel and feasting sad thoughts come;
Youth's years how few, age how sure!

In Praise of Ale

Thomas Bonham

When that the chill Charocco blows
And winter tells a heavy tale,
When pies and daws and rooks and crows
Do sit and curse in frost and snows,
Then give me ale.

Ale in a Saxon rumkin then,
Such as will make Grimalkin prate,
Bids valour burgeon in tall men,
Quickens the poet's wit and pen,
Despises fate.

Ale, that the absent battle fights,
And scorns the march of Swedish drum;
Disputes of princes, laws, and rights;
What's done and past tells mortal wights,
And what's to come.

Ale, that the ploughman's heart up keeps
And equals it to tyrants' thrones;
That wipes the eye that fain would weep,
And lulls in sweet and dainty sleep
The o'erwearied bones.

Grandchild of Ceres, barley's daughter,
Wine's emulous neighbour if but stale,
Ennobling all the nymphs of water
And filling each man's mouth with laughter—
Oh, give me ale!

New Hampshire

T. S. Eliot

Children's voices in the orchard
Between the blossom- and the fruit-time:
Golden head, crimson head,
Between the green tip and the root.
Black wing, brown wing, hover over;
Twenty years and the spring is over;
Today grieves, tomorrow grieves,
Cover me over, light-in-leaves;
Golden head, black wing,
Cling, swing,
Spring, sing,
Swing up into the apple-tree.

The Thrush's Nest

John Clare

Within a thick and spreading hawthorn bush
That overhung a mole-hill large and round,
I heard from morn to morn a merry thrush
Sing hymns to sunrise, while I drank the sound
With joy; and, often an intruding guest,
I watched her secret toils from day to day—
How true she warped the moss to form a nest,
And modelled it within with wood and clay;
And by and by, like heath-bells gilt with dew,
There lay her shining eggs, as bright as flowers,
Ink-spotted over shells of greeny blue;
And there I witnessed, in the sunny hours,
A brood of nature's minstrels chirp and fly,
Glad as that sunshine and the laughing sky.

Snow in the Suburbs

Thomas Hardy

Every branch big with it,
Bent every twig with it,
Every fork like a white web-foot;
Every street and pavement mute:
Some flakes have lost their way, and grope back upward, when
Meeting those meandering down they turn and descend again.
The palings are glued together like a wall,
And there is no waft of wind with the fleecy fall.

A sparrow enters the tree,
Whereupon immediately
A snow-lump thrice his own slight size
Descends on him and showers his head and eyes.
And overturns him,
And near inurns him,
And lights on a nether twig, when its brush
Starts off a volley of other lodging lumps with a rush.

The steps are a blanched slope,
Up which, with feeble hope,
A black cat comes, wide-eyed and thin;
And we take him in.

From 'A Winter's Tale'

William Shakespeare

Lawn as white as driven snow;
Cyprus black as e'er was crow;
Gloves as sweet as damask roses;
Masks for faces and for noses;
Bugle-bracelet, necklace-amber,
Perfume for a lady's chamber;
Golden quoifs and stomachers,
For my lads to give their dears;
Pins and poking-sticks of steel,
What maids lack from head to heel:
Come buy of me, come; come buy, come buy;
Buy, lads, or else your lasses cry
Come buy.

Meeting at Night

Robert Browning

The grey sea and the long black land;
And the yellow half-moon large and low;
And the startled little waves that leap
In fiery ringlets from their sleep,
As I gain the cove with pushing prow,
And quench its speed i' the slushy sand.

Then a mile of warm sea-scented beach;
Three fields to cross till a farm appears;
A tap at the pane, the quick sharp scratch
And blue spurt of a lighted match,
And a voice less loud, thro' its joys and fears,
Than the two hearts beating each to each!

The Song of Shadows

Walter De La Mare

Sweep thy faint strings, Musician,
With thy long lean hand;
Downward the starry tapers burn,
Sinks soft the waning sand;
The old hound whimpers couched in sleep,
The embers smoulder low;
Across the walls the shadows
Come and go.

Sweep softly thy strings, Musician,
The minutes mount to hours;
Frost on the windless casement weaves
A labyrinth of flowers;
Ghosts linger in the darkening air,
Hearken at the open door;
Music hath called them, dreaming,
Home once more.

Love

Ben Jonson

Have you seen but a bright lily grow
Before rude hands have touch'd it?
Have you mark'd but the fall of the snow
Before the soil hath smutch'd it?
Have you felt the wool of beaver,
Or swan's down ever?
Or have smelt o' the bud o' the brier,
Or the nard in the fire?
Or have tested the bag of the bee?
O so white, O so soft, O so sweet is she!

The Lotus-Eaters

Alfred, Lord Tennyson

There is sweet music here that softer falls
Than petals from blown roses on the grass,
Or night-dews on still waters between walls
Of shadowy granite, in a gleaming pass;

Music that gentlier on the spirit lies,
Than tired eyelids upon tired eyes;
Music that brings sweet sleep down from the blissful skies.
Here are cool mosses deep,
And thro' the moss the ivies creep,
And in the stream the long-leaved flowers weep,
And from the craggy ledge the poppy hangs in sleep.

Tintern Abbey

William Wordsworth

The sounding cataract
Haunted me like a passion: the tall rock,
The mountain, and the deep and gloomy wood,
Their colours and their forms, were then to me
An appetite; a feeling and a love,
That had no need of a remoter charm,
By thought supplied, nor any interest
Unborrowed from the eye.—That time is past . . .
For I have learned
To look on nature, not as in the hour
Of thoughtless youth; but hearing often times
The still, sad music of humanity,
Nor harsh nor grating, though of ample power
To chasten and subdue. And I have felt
A presence that disturbs me with the joy
Of elevated thoughts; a sense sublime
Of something far more deeply interfused,
Whose dwelling is the light of setting suns,
And the round ocean and the living air,

And the blue sky, and in the mind of man:
A motion and a spirit that impels
All thinking things, all objects of all thought,
And rolls through all things. Therefore am I still
A lover of the meadows and the woods,
And the mountains; and of all that we behold
From this green earth . . .

Mad Cat

R. J. Pickles

See the mad cat dance,
paw-primed, wide-eyed,
frantic in the moonlit glade.

See him torture tense trees
which stand in solemn queues
like old men round a park bench.

See him dart, slant-eyed,
like a startled fish,
into deep shadow pools.

See him catch, claw-proud,
the bright-eyed mouse
which watched him play too long.

Wind Through Barley

D. O. Pitches

The wind is green
moving palely through the green barley
in long thin sinuous lines advancing
the barley circularly dancing
dipping, spirally rotating lifting.
Over the green field green wind is drifting.

From out the field continual gusts of scent
fill all the air my senses touch with dust
with all the powdery dust of unswept fields
the dry and chaffy last year's threshing scent,
a dry smell reinforced by memory, which
smothers the new damp grass smell in the ditch,
and through the odourless long-dead white grasses
from the threshing floor the powdery thin wind passes.

Eclipse

Carl Inglis

Wide rippling water of Atlantic seas,
Grey-clouded, dark and deep beneath the waves,
Slumber like melted lead beneath the moon.

Deep sapphire blue of daylit ocean,
White stippled sky above white-crested waves,
Meeting and melting in the solar flame.

White haunting clouds above the desert sea,
Mist-shrouded islands, built of lunar stone;
Sun and moon eclipse, sky and sea are one.

After School

J. D. Goodger

a playing field of feet everywhere
slurred in the new snow and
just left about for the sun to weak
on
The foot makers are all gone now
gulped up by buses
   It was some manypede from the Ice Age
   grinning at January
   that shed all these feet
   (while no one was looking)
Soon a little man with a pointed stick and a pulled-out shadow
will come out
and prod at them, etc.
and spear them all up
and stuff them in a sack.

Bare Almond Trees

D. H. Lawrence

Wet almond-trees, in the rain,
Like iron sticking grimly out of earth;
Black almond trunks, in the rain,
Like iron implements, twisted, hideous out of the earth,
Out of the deep, soft fledge of Sicilian winter-green,
Earth-grass uneatable,
Almond trunks curving blackly, iron-dark, climbing the slopes.

Almond-tree, beneath the terrace rail,
Black, rusted, iron trunk,
You have welded your thin stems finer,
Like steel, like sensitive steel in the air,
Grey, lavender, sensitive steel, curving thinly and brittly up in
    a parabola.

What are you doing in the December rain?
Have you a strange electric sensitiveness in your steel tips?
Do you feel the air for electric influences
Like some strange magnetic apparatus?
Do you take in messages, in some strange code,
From heaven's wolfish, wandering electricity, that prowls so
    constantly round Etna?

Do you take the whisper of sulphur from the air?
Do you hear the chemical accents of the sun?
Do you telephone the roar of the waters over the earth?
And from all this, do you make calculations?
Sicily, December's Sicily in a mass of rain
With iron branching blackly, rusted like old, twisted
    implements
And brandishing and stooping over earth's wintry fledge,
    climbing the slopes
Of uneatable soft green!

Under the Pier

John Walsh

High up among the girders of the pier,
Under the dark planking of the pier,
They perch and sing:
A boy with tarry legs, and lower,
A girl in blue jeans.
Suddenly he leaps—
Heedless of us beneath him,
Heedless of twisted ankle and broken bones—
And with a whoop comes clattering down among the stones.

The Anemone

John Walsh

Under this ledge of rock a brown
And soft anemone clings,
Spreading his fingers to the sea
Deliciously.
I kneel down on the sand,
And squeezing gently with my thumb
I loose his hold and take him in my hand.
But now how swift his fingers are withdrawn!—
His tendrils shrunk and gone!
I dabble him and water him in vain—
He will not flower again;
And though I press him firmly to his rock,
He will not stick again or cling,
But sinks disconsolately down,
And is lost, poor thing!

Alarm

Joan Prince

Elms are etched against the clean washed sky.
Rooks perch
Like black fruit on brittle branches,
Silent and somnolent.

Suddenly,
In a swarming, squawking flurry they scatter,
As though some giant had plunged
Both hands into the tree
And flung them up to heaven in sullen anger.
They wheel and bank in tortuous turmoil,
Panic-stricken yet aggressive,
Each wing-beat aimless, but controlled
By instinctive balanced beauty.
Then swiftly the black squadrons
Dip and dive into the elms.
The raucous cacophony ceases abruptly.

Elms are etched against the clean washed sky.
Rooks perch
Like black fruit on brittle branches,
Silent and somnolent.

Fern Hill

Dylan Thomas

Now as I was young and easy under the apple boughs
About the lilting house and happy as the grass was green,
The night above the dingle starry,
Time let me hail and climb
Golden in the heydays of his eyes,
And honoured among wagons I was prince of the apple towns
And once below a time I lordly had the trees and leaves
Trail with daisies and barley
Down the rivers of the windfall light.

And as I was green and carefree, famous among the barns
About the happy yard and singing as the farm was home,
In the sun that is young once only,
Time let me play and be
Golden in the mercy of his means,
And green and golden I was huntsman and herdsman, the
    calves
Sang to my horn, the foxes on the hills barked clear and cold,
And the sabbath rang slowly
In the pebbles of the holy streams.

All the sun long it was running, it was lovely, the hay
Fields high as the house, the tunes from the chimneys, it was
    air
And playing, lovely and watery
And fire green as grass.
And nightly under the simple stars
As I rode to sleep the owls were bearing the farm away,
All the moon long I heard, blessed among stables, the nightjars
Flying with the ricks, and the horses
Flashing into the dark.

And then to awake, and the farm, like a wanderer white
With the dew, come back, the cock on his shoulder: it was all
Shining, it was Adam and maiden,
The sky gathered again
And the sun grew round that very day.
So it must have been after the birth of the simple light
In the first, spinning place, the spellbound horses walking
     warm
Out of the whinnying green stable
On to the fields of praise.

And honoured among foxes and pheasants by the gay house
Under the new made clouds and happy as the heart was long,
In the sun born over and over,
I ran my heedless ways,
My wishes raced through the house high hay
And nothing I cared, at my sky blue trades, that time allows
In all his tuneful turning so few and such morning songs
Before the children green and golden
Follow him out of grace.

Nothing I cared, in the lamb white days, that time would
     take me
Up to the swallow thronged loft by the shadow of my hand,
In the moon that is always rising,
Nor that riding to sleep
I should hear him fly with the high fields
And wake tó the farm forever fled from the childless land.
Oh as I was young and easy in the mercy of his means,
Time held me green and dying
Though I sang in my chains like the sea.

Underground

Rose Macaulay

A sultry, small, perpetual breeze drives, sickly-sweet and warm
    and thin,
Charged with ozone and oxygen, like to a wind from summer
    seas,
Down smooth white grooves, all roseate with gaudy tints of
    tropic flowers,
Down shining lanes gay as the bowers of merry moles, and
    decorates
With red-lipped maids and azure woods and storied rhyme
    and pictured tale
Of brilliant, hectic things for sale, and pantomime, and
    wondrous foods.
Did ever such gay and lovely holes lie tunnelled deep beneath
    grey skies?
These lanes would sure be paradise for a king plutocrat of
    moles.

Like the morning sea running up a river-bed
The tide drives in.
It surges and brims stormily
With a goblin din,
As of wrestlers wrestling for places
Where few places are;
And the guardian gnomes chant, 'Right down
The centre of the car!'
The upper world is all forgot: these are the people of a dream,
Flowing like fish on a strong stream through deep pale caves
    where suns are not.
These are a people wild and dumb, and two things only do
    they know—

Whence they come and whither they go; but why they go and
    why they come,
Or why they e'er should move at all, is hidden from their
    cloudless eyes
That stare aloof, in chill surprise, on others following the call.

Food on Board Ship

Hilaire Belloc

I said a little while ago
The food was very much below
The standard needed to prepare
Explorers for the special fare
Which all authorities declare
Is needful in the tropics.
A Frenchman sitting next to us
Rejected the asparagus;
The turtle soup was often cold,
The ices hot, the omelettes old,
The coffee worse than I can tell;
And Sin (who had a happy knack
Of rhyming rapidly and well
Like Cyrano de Bergerac)
Said 'Quant à moi, je n'aime pas
Du tout ce pâté de foie gras!'
But this fastidious taste
Succeeded in a startling way;
At Dinner on the following day
They gave us Bloater Paste.
Well-hearty pioneers and rough
Should not be over nice;

I think these lines are quite enough,
And hope they will suffice
To make the Caterers observe
The kind of person whom they serve.

Sowing

Edward Thomas

It was a perfect day
For sowing; just
As sweet and dry was the ground
As tobacco-dust.

I tasted deep the hour
Between the far
Owl's chuckling first soft cry
And the first star.

A long stretched hour it was;
Nothing undone
Remained; the early seeds
All safely sown.

And now, hark at the rain,
Windless and light,
Half a kiss, half a tear,
Saying good-night.

Hands

W. W. Gibson

Tempest without; within, the mellow glow
Of mingling lamp and firelight over all—
Etchings and water colours on the wall,
Cushions and curtains of clear indigo,
Rugs, damask-red and blue as Tyrian seas,
Deep chairs, black oaken settles, hammered brass,
Translucent porcelain and sea-green glass—
Colour and warmth and light and dreamy ease;

And I sit wondering where are now the hands
That wrought at anvil, easel, wheel, and loom—
Hands, slender, swart, red, gnarled—in foreign lands
Or English shops to furnish this seemly room;
And all the while, without, the windy rain
Drums like dead fingers tapping at the pane.

Dolphins in Blue Water

Amy Lowell

Hey! Crackerjack—jump!
Blue water,
Pink water,
Swirl, flick, flitter;
Snout into a wave-trough,
Plunge, curl.
Bow over,
Under,
Razor-cut and tumble.

Roll, turn—
Straight—and shoot at the sky,
All rose-flame drippings.
Down ring,
Drop,
Nose under,
Hoop,
Tail,
Dive,
And gone;
With smooth over-swirlings of blue water,
Oil-smooth cobalt,
Slipping, liquid lapis lazuli,
Emerald shadings,
Tintings of pink and ochre.
Prismatic slidings
Underneath a windy sky.

Who Whistled?

Richard Church

Someone was whistling.
Who was it? Who was it?
Of the passing faces,
The tired brains?
Where was the demon of merriment lodged?

Over the drumming of the City,
Over the yawn of the lunch hour,
Over the pounding of the heatwave,
The boy-flute rose;
A lark from the dew,
A cup from the well,
A gift from a child.

It poised,
Trembled;
Poised,
And fell.
And the buses ramped on,
And the faces closed.
And the brains slept,
In the City.

In Lamplight

Martin Armstrong

Now that the chill October day is declining,
Pull the blinds, draw each voluminous curtain,
Till the room is full of gloom and of the uncertain
Gleams of firelight on polished edges shining.
Then bring the rosy lamp to its wonted station
On the dark-gleaming table. In that soft splendour
Well-known things of the room, grown deep and tender,
Gather round, a mysterious congregation:
Pallid sheen of the silver, the bright brass fender,
The wine-red pool of carpet, the bowl of roses,

Lustrous-hearted, crimsons and purples looming
From dusky rugs and curtains. Nothing discloses
The unseen walls, but the broken, richly-glooming
Gold of frames and opulent wells of mingling
Dim colours gathered in darkened mirrors. And breaking
The dreamlike spell, and your deep chair forsaking,
You go, perhaps, to the shelves, and, slowly singling
Some old rich-blazoned book, return. But the gleaming
Spells close round you again and you fall to dreaming,
Eyes grown dim, the book on your lap unheeded.

Statue of a Miner

Ernest Rhys

Let it be marble, but as black
As coal; and give him mighty thews,
Broad shoulder-blades, Achilles' back,
And arms that tighten while he hews.
A clean-shaved face, and shrewd enough;
Short legs; a torso strong as stone;
Scarred cheeks, square chin, and features rough
As if the man were quarry-hewn.
And stubborn? Purse the under-lip
To look as obdurate as you can—
He learnt that from his iron grip
Upon the pick. But mole or man,
He has his weakness, like us all:
Let it be clay—his pedestal.

The Line-Gang

Robert Frost

Here comes the line-gang pioneering by.
They throw a forest down less cut than broken.
They plant dead trees for living, and the dead
They string together with a living thread.
They string an instrument against the sky
Wherein words, whether beaten out or spoken,
Will run as hushed as when they were a thought.
But in no hush they string it: they go past
With shouts afar to pull the cable taut,
To hold it hard until they make it fast,
To ease away—they have it. With a laugh
And oath of towns that set the wild at naught,
They bring the telephone and the telegraph.

Gipsies

John Clare

The gipsies seek wide sheltering woods again,
With droves of horses flock to mark their lane,
And trample on dead leaves, and hear the sound,
And look and see the black clouds gather round,
And set their camps, and free from muck and mire,
And gather stolen sticks to make the fire.
The roasted hedgehog, bitter though as gall,
Is eaten up and relished by them all.
They know the woods and every fox's den
And get their living far away from men;

The shooters ask them where to find the game,
The rabbits know them and are almost tame.
The aged women, tawny with the smoke,
Go with the winds and crack the rotted oak.

Dawn

John Masefield

The dawn comes cold: the haystack smokes,
The green twigs crackle in the fire,
The dew is dripping from the oaks,
And sleepy men bear milking-yokes
Slowly towards the cattle-byre.

Down in the town a clock strikes six,
The grey east heaven burns and glows,
The dew shines on the thatch of ricks,
A slow old crone comes gathering sticks,
The red cock in the ox-yard crows.

Beyond the stack where we have lain
The road runs twisted like a snake
(The white road to the land of Spain),
The road that we must foot again,
Though the feet halt and the heart ache.

The Emigrants

Clifford Dyment

The ship strained at the hawsers. Through the fog
Sounded the thud of iron on wooden wharf,
Rattle of chain and slap of sullen sea.
The throats of distant ships wailed for the light.

We who had hoped to sail paced narrow decks,
Blind and bewildered at this dark delay.

The Winnowers

Robert Bridges

Betwixt two billows of the downs
The little hamlet lies,
And nothing sees but the bald crowns
Of the hills, and the blue skies.

Clustering beneath the long descent
And grey slopes of the wold,
The red roofs nestle, oversprent
With lichen yellow as gold.

We found it in the mid-day sun
Basking, what time of year
The thrush his singing has begun,
Ere the first leaves appear.

High from his load a woodman pitched
His faggots on the stack:
Knee-deep in straw the cattle twitched
Sweet hay from crib and rack:

And from the barn hard by was borne
A steady muffled din,
By which we knew that threshed corn
Was winnowing, and went in.

The sunbeams on the motey air
Streamed through the open door,
And on the brown arms moving bare,
And the grain upon the floor.

One turns the crank, one stoops to feed
The hopper, lest it lack,
One in the bushel scoops the seed,
One stands to hold the sack.

We watched the good grain rattle down,
And the awns fly in the draught;
To see us both so pensive grown
The honest labourers laughed:

Merry they were, because the wheat
Was clean and plump and good,
Pleasant to hand and eye, and meet
For market and for food.

It chanced we from the city were,
And had not gat us free
In spirit from the store and stir
Of its immensity.

But here we found ourselves again
Where humble harvests bring
After much toil but little grain,
'Tis merry winnowing.

First Spring Morning

Robert Bridges

Look! Look! the spring it comes;
O feel the gentle air,
That wanders thro' the boughs to burst
The thick buds everywhere!
The birds are glad to see
The high unclouded sun:
Winter is fled away, they sing,
The gay time is begun.

Adown the meadows green
Let us go dance and play,
And look for violets in the lane,
And ramble far away
To gather primroses,
That in the woodland grow,
And hunt for oxslips, or if yet
The blades of bluebells show:

There the old woodman gruff
Hath half the coppice cut,
And weaves the hurdles all day long
Beside his willow hut.
We'll steal on him, and then
Startle him, all with glee
Singing our song of winter fled
And summer soon to be.

Sonnet

Thomas Hood

Time was I liked a cheesecake well enough,
All human children have a sweetish taste;
I used to revel in a pie, or puff,
Or tart—we all were Tartars in our youth;
To meet with jam or jelly was good luck,
All candies most complacently I crumped,
A stick of liquorice was good to suck,
And sugar was as often liked as lumped!
On treacle's 'linked sweetness long drawn out',
Or honey I could feast like any fly;
I thrilled when lollipops were hawked about;
How pleased to compass hard-bake or bulls' eye;
How charmed if Fortune in my power cast
Elecampane—but that campaign is past.

Smelling the End of Green July

Peter Yates

Smelling the end of green July
I entered through spiked gates a London park
To grill my body in the sun,
And to untie thought's parcel of pure dark
Under the blue gaze of the candid sky.

The air was heavy, without breath;
The asphalt paths gave off a hollow ring;
And wearing haloes of shrill birds
The Statues watched the flowers withering,
And leaves curl up for Summer's rusty death.

A zoo-like sameness of all parks!
The grasses lick the railings of wrought-iron,
And chains clink in the shrubbery
As Summer roaring like a shabby lion
Claws at the meaning of the human marks.

I saw the tops of buses wheel
Geranium flashes over pigeon-walls;
And heard the rocket-cries of children
Fly upwards, bursting where the water calls,
And scissors sunlight with a glint of steel.

The wings of slowly dripping light
Pulled boats across a swan-enlightened lake;
And near youth's skipping-ropes of joy
I felt the strings of my old parcel break,
Spilling its cold abstractions with delight.

I watched the game of life begun
Among dead matches, droppings of the birds;
And left thought's parcel on a bench
While I relearned the flight of singing words
Under the blowlamp kisses of the sun.

Radio

A. S. J. Tessimond

Here is another dream, another forgetting, another doorway:
Sound, to drown the sting of the rain on the pane and the
        sough of the wind
And the sound of the sea:
Sound, like feathers, to muffle the sound of silence
And the beat of the heart:

Sound to go with you, through the valley of the shadow in the
    dashboard of the shining car:
The comfortable voice of the announcer purring the ruin of
    kingdoms,
The fall of cities and the fall of wickets,
The random dead and the New Year knights:
Sound like a sea to conceal the bone, the broken shell, the
    broken ship.

The Wound

Charles Martin
(aged 11)

It was not
Like most wounds
Red, gaping, slowly
Oozing hot blood.

If it did have a colour
It was blue, green,
Grey and black all mixed
Oozing wickedness.

Cold, murderous
Yet burning with rage
It grew superhumanly
Out of sight.

It got inside things
People and animals
And crept under cover
Through the dark fog.

Through the mist
And darkness went the blue wound,
The wounded, insulted spirit
Wickedly searching for vengeance.

Fish and Chips

A. Elliott-Cannon

Fish and chips today for tea,
A fish for Gran, a fish for me.
I buy them at the corner place,
From smiling Meg of rosy face.

Meg sees the small boys lick their lips
At battered fish and golden chips.
Her apron's white, her hands are red;
She sees the hungry thousands fed.

For sixpence more there're peas as well,
Mushy peas with gorgeous smell;
And butter beans on Friday night,
Pale, steaming beans for your delight.

The counter's white, the walls are pink,
The shelves hold lemonade to drink.
The fat is hissing in the pan,
And soon I hurry home to Gran.

The chips look good; they taste the same;
They've won our Meg some local fame.
Fish and chips today for tea,
A fish for Gran, a fish for me.

The Fog

W. H. Davies

I saw the fog grow thick,
Which soon made blind my ken;
It made tall men of boys,
And giants of tall men.

It clutched my throat, I coughed;
Nothing was in my head
Except two heavy eyes
Like balls of burning lead.

And when it grew so black
That I could know no place,
I lost all judgment then,
Of distance and of space.

The street lamps, and the lights
Upon the halted cars,
Could either be on earth
Or be the heavenly stars.

A man passed by me close;
I asked my way; he said,
'Come, follow me, my friend'—
I followed where he led.

He rapped the stones in front,
'Trust me,' he said, 'and come';
I followed like a child—
A blind man led me home.

Harvest Festival

Peter Mullineaux
(aged 13)

Bread, golden, crispy, curled and
Sculptured into intricate shapes.
Sniff the clean baked fragrance,
Long to break off that tiny, sharp,
Knobbly corner.
And let it melt on the tongue,
Tasting delicious.

Flowers piled high,
Gorgeous explosions of colour,
Russet apples, amber, yellow,
Crimson blazing.
Black frosty grapes,
Cabbages, green-leaved, crimped,
And earthy,
Festival of food as summer fades.

Pleasant Sounds

John Clare

The rustling of leaves under the feet in woods and under hedges;
The crumping of cat-ice and snow down wood-rides, narrow
    lanes, and every street causeway;
Rustling through a wood or rather rushing, while the wind
    halloos in the oak-top like thunder;
The rustle of birds' wings startled from their nests or flying
    unseen into the bushes;

The whizzing of larger birds overhead in a wood, such as
    crows, puddocks, buzzards;
The trample of robins and woodlarks on the brown leaves, and
    the patter of squirrels on the green moss;
The fall of an acorn on the ground, the pattering of nuts on
    the hazel branches as they fall from ripeness;
The flirt of the groundlark's wing from the stubbles—how
    sweet such pictures on dewy mornings, when the dew
    flashes from its brown feathers!

Things Men have Made

D. H. Lawrence

Things men have made with wakened hands, and put soft life
into are awake through years with transferred touch, and go
on glowing for long years.
And for this reason, some old things are lovely
warm still with the life of forgotten men who made them.

Swift Things are Beautiful

Elizabeth Coatsworth

Swift things are beautiful:
Swallows and deer,
And lightning that falls
Bright veined and clear,
Rivers and meteors,
Wind in the wheat,
The strong-withered horse,
The runner's sure feet.

And slow things are beautiful:
The closing of day,
The pause of the wave
That curves downward to spray,
The ember that crumbles,
The opening flower,
And the ox that moves on
In the quiet of power.

Apples

Laurie Lee

Behold the apples' rounded worlds:
juice-green of July rain,
the black polestar of flower, the rind
mapped with its crimson stain.

The russet, crab, and cottage red
burn to the sun's hot brass,
then drop like sweat from every branch
and bubble in the grass.

They lie as wanton as they fall,
and where they fall and break,
the stallion clamps his crunching jaws,
the starling stabs his beak.

In each plump gourd the cidery bite
of boy's teeth tears the skin;
the waltzing wasp consumes his share,
the bent worm enters in.

And I, with as easy hunger, take
entire my season's dole;
and welcome the ripe, the sweet, the sour,
the hollow and the whole.

When you walk in a Field

James Stephens

When you walk in a field
Look down,
Lest you trample
A daisy's crown,

But in a city
Look always high,
And watch
The beautiful clouds go by.

Smells

Christopher Morley

Why is it that the poets tell
So little of the smell?
These are the odours I love well:

The smell of coffee freshly ground;
Or rich plum pudding, holly crowned;
Or onions fried and deeply browned.

The fragrance of a fumy pipe;
The smell of apples, newly ripe;
And printers' ink on leaden type.

Woods by moonlight in September
Breathe most sweet; and I remember
Many a smoky camp-fire ember.

Camphor, turpentine, and tea,
The balsam of a Christmas tree,
These are whiffs of gramarye. . . .
A ship smells best of all to me!

Skating

William Wordsworth

And in the frosty season, when the sun
Was set, and visible for many a mile
The cottage windows blazed through twilight gloom,
I heeded not their summons: happy time
It was indeed for all of us—for me
It was a time of rapture. Clear and loud
The village clock tolled six—I wheeled about,
Proud and exulting like an untired horse
That cares not for his home. All shod with steel,
We hissed along the polished ice in games
Confederate, imitative of the chase
And woodland pleasures—the resounding horn,
The pack loud chiming, and the hunted hare.
So through the darkness and the cold we flew,
And not a voice was idle; with the din
Smitten, the precipices rang aloud;

The leafless trees and every icy crag
Tinkled like iron; while far-distant hills
Into the tumult sent an alien sound
Of melancholy not unnoticed, while the stars
Eastward were sparkling clear, and in the west
The orange sky of evening died away.

If I had a Hammer

Lee Hays and Pete Seeger

If I had a hammer,
I'd hammer in the morning,
I'd hammer in the evening,
All over this land;
I'd hammer out danger,
I'd hammer out a warning,
I'd hammer out love between all of my brothers,
All over this land.

If I had a bell,
I'd ring it in the morning,
I'd ring it in the evening,
All over this land;
I'd ring out danger,
I'd ring out a warning,
I'd ring out love between all of my brothers,
All over this land.

If I had a song,
I'd sing it in the morning,
I'd sing it in the evening,
All over this land;
I'd sing out danger,
I'd sing out a warning,
I'd sing out love between all of my brothers,
All over this land.

Well, I've got a hammer,
And I've got a bell,
And I've got a song to sing
All over this land;
It's a hammer of justice,
It's a bell of freedom,
It's a song above love between all of my brothers,
All over this land.

The National English Meal

Linda Hughes
(aged 14)

The taste of fresh-fried filleted fish:
Not the scraggy scraps from a stinted stock,
Nor a slimy slice from a smog-smelly shop,
But sizzling, succulent, sea-fresh fish.
And choicest, crispy, chunky chips:
Not pans of pallid, prostrate pulp,
Nor charred chunks, or withered wisps,
But crispy, chunky, sizzling, succulent, purely
English fish and chips.

From: 'Under Milk Wood'

Dylan Thomas

NARRATOR: There's the clip clop of horses on the sunhoneyed cobbles of the humming streets, hammering of horse-shoes, gobble quack and cackle, tomtit twitter from the bird-ounced boughs, braying on Donkey Down. Bread is baking, pigs are grunting, chop goes the butcher, milk-churns bell, tills ring, sheep cough, dogs shout, saws sing. Oh the Spring whinny and morning moo from the clog dancing farms, the gulls' gab and rabble on the boat-bobbing river and sea and the cockles bubbling in the sand, scamper of sanderlings, curlew cry, crow caw, pigeon coo, clock strike, bull bellow, and the ragged gabble of the beargarden school as the women scratch and babble in Mrs Organ Morgan's general shop where everything is sold: custard, buckets, henna, rat-traps, shrimp-nets, sugar, stamps, confetti, paraffin, hatchets, whistles.

Morning Thanksgiving

John Drinkwater

Thank God for sleep in the long quiet night,
For the clear day calling through the little leaded panes,
For the shining well-water and the warm golden light,
And the paths washed white by singing rains.

We thank Thee, O God, for exultation born
Of the kiss of Thy winds, for life among the leaves,
For the whirring wings that pass about the wonder of the
    morn,
For the changing plumes of swallows gliding upwards to their
    eaves.

For the treasure of the garden, the gillyflowers of gold,
The prouder petalled tulips, the primrose full of spring,
For the crowded orchard boughs, and the swelling buds that
    hold
A yet unwoven wonder, to Thee our praise we bring.

Thank God for good bread, for the honey in the comb,
For the brown-shelled eggs, for the clustered blossoms set
Beyond the open window in a pink and cloudy foam,
For the laughing lovers among the branches met.

For the kind-faced women we bring our thanks to Thee,
With shapely mothering arms and grave eyes clear and blithe,
For the tall young men, strong-thewed as men may be,
For the old man bent above his scythe.

For earth's little secret and innumerable ways,
For the carol and the colour, Lord, we bring
What things may be of thanks, and that Thou hast lent our
    days
Eyes to see and ears to hear and lips to sing.

The Evening Comes

Matthew Arnold

> The evening comes, the fields are still,
> The tinkle of the thirsty rill,
> Unheard all day, ascends again;
> Deserted is the half-mown plain,
> Silent the swaths! the ringing wain,
> The mower's cry, the dog's alarms,
> All housed within the sleeping farms!

The business of the day is done,
The last-left haymaker is gone.
And from the thyme upon the height,
And from the elder-blossom white
And pale dog-roses in the hedge,
And from the mint-plant in the sedge,
In puffs of balm the night-air blows
The perfume which the day forgoes.
And on the pure horizon far,
See, pulsing with the first-born star,
The liquid sky above the hill!
The evening comes, the fields are still.